BESIDE
STILL WATERS

Finding Rest, Refreshment, and Restoration for Your Soul

21-Day Devotional

LEONIE H. MATTISON, ED.D.

WELCOME
TO BESIDE STILL WATERS!

This devotional is dedicated to women who have survived the soul-crushing reality, pain, and impact of abuse. I'm so glad you've chosen to join me for twenty-one days to finding rest, refreshment, and restoration for your soul by the still waters.

This is part of the Thread collection which consists of the main Thread book, this devotional, an adult coloring book, and an audio tape. Each can be used separately in your spiritual healing process. But better still, they can also be used simultaneously to support the transformative process, as one reinforces the other.

Read the book and do the exercises required, listen to the audio book to remind yourself that others have also suffered as you have. Use this devotional in the morning or during the day as a reminder of the path to healing you have chosen. Color in the adult coloring book to start designing your best self.

My prayer is that the stories, the sharing of my life story and the six steps of the THREAD will work to bring peace, healing, and restoration to your life and a profoundly greater intimacy with God.

I've designed these twenty-one days of Scripture verses, prayers, and exercises to help you rest in God's love, stop reliving the past, and continue pressing into God and His Word. Then you will move forward in power and might.

This devotional is all about you. It's your time to shut out the world and be intentional about finding rest, refreshment, and restoration. Think of these twenty-one days as your personal retreat with God. Don't pack anything. Leave it all behind as you pursue healing from physical, emotional, sexual, and/or spiritual abuse.

"Come!" Anyone who is thirsty should come to Jesus. He will give the water of true life to anyone who wants it. They will not have to pay anything for it"
Revelation 22:17 EASY

May you find wholeness in God as you rest your heart, quiet your soul, and meditate on the refreshing and restorative life-giving Word of Truth.

Leonie Mattison

ACKNOWLEDGMENTS

Thank you to my mother, Joy May Lawrence. It was you who introduced me to the Lord and taught me that, no matter what life throws my way, I can call on Jesus anytime of the day, especially in the morning. Thank you, Mommy!

I also want to thank God and everyone who empowered, inspired, and supported me throughout this journey. I appreciate you all.

Table
of Contents

WEEK THREE

SOME TIPS
FOR USING THIS
DEVOTIONAL

This twenty-one-day devotional is to help you focus on tapping into your Spirit-led power and resources. This will help you decide on the direction of your life and achieve the results you want to accomplish. I believe that when we know what we don't want, we can give full attention to coming into alignment with what we do want. To become a deliberate creator, it's important to set the tone for seeking and becoming one with God, refueling your faith, and empowering your resolve to complete this devotional.

To set things in motion, I've provided instructions below to guide your journey. Each day, we'll be digging into Scripture to focus our study for the day. Prayerfully read the selected "Key Verses" and personalize the Word of God when you read it.

Next, tap in to the "Thoughts on Today's Verse," then, to hone your focus, connect to God through "Prayer" and ask Him for what you want. It's crucial that you take time to quiet your mind. When your mind settles down, listen to God's response to what you've requested.

To guide yourself to a new result, speak aloud the "Personal Declaration" as you allow the manifestation of your request. Remember, the happier you are, the better things will flow.

Finally, "Take Soul Care Actions" to help you identify the beliefs and habits you want to keep, release, and establish to achieve your vision of success. Be sure to take "Time For Self-Reflection."

Here are a few things that will help you develop a routine or improve the one you already faithfully use:

- **Decide** what results you want from this devotional (for example, to hear from God about a specific issue you're facing) and write it down.

- **Prepare** and plan a set time to meet with the Lord. Adjust distractions such as social media, TV, etc. If necessary, set an alarm on your device so you'll be reminded. Keep your time doable and make sure it works for you. Make any adjustments to improve on your routine.

- **Create** your own "quiet oasis" where you meet with the Lord on a regular basis (in your home, in your car, in a park). One of mine is my lazy chair by the window. I love sunlight, so it's the perfect place. I have a little end table, a plant, a lamp, my iPad (for music), my Bible, my journal, and my devotional material. Everything is right there, so I can meet with the Lord each morning.

- **Get** into Scripture and see what the Lord has to say to you in the Key Verse. Then focus on how to apply that verse to your life, and be sure to hold on to the Word in your spirit and feel the joy of the Lord with daily affirmation.

- **Use** your prayer journal to surrender things to God, then write in your journal. Finally, plan what you'll accomplish in the day. You can practice these steps each day (or whatever routine you establish).

Remember, this is your time to learn from the Lord and become consistent in seeking and delighting yourself in Him; He will give you your heart's desires (Psalm 37:4). Follow these simple daily instructions as you spend time pressing into God:

STEP 1:

Read today's devotion in your quiet time.

STEP 2:

Ask the Holy Spirit
to reveal what God wants you to know through His Word.

STEP 3:

Receive God's instructions.

STEP 4:

Live out loud what you read in your daily life.

ADDITIONALLY, YOU CAN:

STEP 5:

Purchase the audio version of this devotional on my website at
www.leoniemattison.com.

STEP 6:

Join our Facebook Group and share with others
what you're learning and feel free
to post your thoughts in the comments section at
https://www.facebook.com/LeonieMattisonOfficial

STEP 7:

Join **"Yes to Intentional Transformation"** a yearlong learning journey where you **connect** with other like-minded women, receive live group **monthly mentoring** from me, weekly **transformation tips**, and year-end retreat that offer you the chance to disconnect, reflect, and celebrate your accomplishments.

WEEK 1

FIND REST

Your life is a beautiful masterpiece you get to co-create with God.

Leonie H. Mattison

Day 1

TAKE YOUR BURDEN TO THE LORD

Key Verse

"Come to me, all of you who are tired and have heavy loads, and I will give you rest. Accept my teachings and learn from me, because I am gentle and humble in spirit, and you will find rest for your lives. The burden that I ask you to accept is easy; the load I give you to carry is light."

(Matthew 11:28–30 NCV)

THOUGHTS
ON TODAY'S KEY VERSE

Have you ever shown up somewhere uninvited? You knock on the door, waiting for an answer and hoping that you'll be let in. We often take the same approach with God. We come to Him in our times of desperation, beating on the door of His heart in our weariness, desiring rest.

My sister, you're not a stranger showing up at God's door unwanted. Therefore, you can expect Him to respond. I know many people have caused you to feel unwelcome or unimportant, but that is completely opposite of how God feels about you. He has invited you to rest beside the still waters, and with the warmest of welcomes, He says, "Come to me."

Jesus has offered you His yoke; it's an offering of oneness, partnership, freedom from shame and guilt, and connection to the heart and love of God. The yoke of God is His understanding, peace, truth, promises, rest, love, and knowledge. You can think of it as a care package from God to you, His beloved.

God is saying to you, "Daughter, let me help you. Why are you trying to do everything on your own?" As the yolk of an egg is one with the egg itself, you are one with God. He knows that you're unable to enter his rest by your own strength, so He's offering to help you. 'He's calling you into oneness with Him so that He can teach you how to rest in His presence.

But how do you come to God and give Him your burdens? By following as the Holy Spirit guides you to the still waters. Get alone with God, tell Him your troubles, and then release them to Him in faith, knowing He'll help you—because He will!

He'll carry your burdens as He leads you in His ways. It's there that you'll find rest. Not rest as the world gives, which only benefits the body. God provides real rest that allows your soul to let go of everything that weighs it down.

The burdens will be released, and for the first time in a long while, you'll breathe the breath of deliverance, allowing Jesus to carry the weight as you enter His promise of rest.

PRAYER

God, I'm not sure if I know how to give You my burdens. I've been carrying them for so long. Many times I've trusted others for help and ended up hurt. So, forgive me if I'm fearful. Despite my reservations, here I am. I'm accepting Your invitation to come close, asking that You help me. Help me to give You all of my hurt, my sorrow, my shame, and my guilt. Father, I give it to You, taking a leap of faith and trusting that You'll bring me into oneness with You. Father, teach me Your ways and embrace me with Your humble and gentle heart so that I may find rest in You. In Jesus' name, I pray, amen.

Personal Declaration

I am one with God and can trust Him with my burdens.

Take Soul Care Actions

1. What things have been preventing you from finding rest, especially the ones that you think about often?

   _____

   _____

   _____

2. What beliefs and habits do you want to keep, release, and establish today?

   • Keep: _____

   • Release: _____

   • Establish: _____

Date:

TIME FOR
SELF-REFLECTION:

_____

_____

_____

_____

_____

_____

_____

_____

_____

_____

_____

_____

_____

_____

_____

_____

_____

_____

_____

_____

_____

_____

_____

_____

_____

_____

_____

_____

_____

_____

_____

_____

_____

_____

_____

_____

_____

_____

_____

_____

Day 2

Safety from the Storm

Key Verse

Those who live in the shelter of the Most High will find rest in the shadow of the Almighty. This I declare about the LORD: He alone is my refuge, my place of safety; He is my God, and I trust in Him.

(Psalm 91:1–2 NLT)

THOUGHTS ON TODAY'S KEY VERSE

Where have you been seeking safety during life's storms? If you're anything like me, you've sought shelter wherever you could find it, whether that place was healthy for you or not.

No one wants to be left out in the rain, right? You're standing outside and, without warning, a storm rolls in. The rain falls, leaving every part of you drenched. Your hair is dripping, and your clothes are heavy from the weight of the downpour. Lightning shoots from the clouds, and thunder roars through the sky like a lion seeking vengeance. And there you are, standing alone—no raincoat, no umbrella, not even a hood. Unprotected, your only choice is to seek shelter in the nearest place of safety.

The presence of God is the only place we are indeed safe. At times my lack of safety has kept me up at night. Rest was far from me. I didn't know then that in the shadow of the Almighty is where rest is found. If you've been drenched by the storms of this life, shelter awaits you by the still waters of the Father's assurance.

Like a mother bird covering her young with her wings, so does your Father cover and shelter you from the storms of life.

Seeking shelter in the wrong places only further jeopardizes your rest and well-being. God's best is that we live in the shelter of the Most High. Here's where we're protected, where true refuge is found, and where true rest is given.

Don't just visit: live on the calm waters. Take up residence there. Get comfortable in the presence of God, trusting Him to be your safeguard, so that you find rest.

PRAYER

Father, I'll be honest: In the past I've sought out shelter in the wrong places. But this time I'm choosing to live in Your shelter. I've been through many storms in my life and now realize I don't have to go through them alone. I will trust that You will be a place of safety, as You have promised, giving me respite when I need it most. As I come in out of the rain, I seek your covering and find rest in Your faithfulness. In Jesus' name, I pray, amen.

Personal
Declaration

I am protected when I rest in the shelter of the Almighty.

Take Soul Care Actions

1. What are some ways and places that you have been seeking shelter?

   _____

   _____

   _____

2. What beliefs and habits do you want to keep, release, and establish today?

   • Keep: _____

   • Release: _____

   • Establish: _____

Date:

TIME FOR SELF-REFLECTION:

_____

_____

_____

_____

_____

_____

_____

_____

_____

_____

_____

_____

_____

_____

_____

_____

_____

_____

DAY 3

DON'T GO ALONE

KEY VERSE

The LORD replied, "I will personally go with you, Moses, and I will give you rest—everything will be fine for you."

(Exodus 33:14 NLT)

Thoughts on Today's Key Verse

Has fear ever kept you from moving forward? Women all over the world are stuck in abusive relationships. They're suffering physical, emotional, sexual, and spiritual abuse in silence because fear has hindered them from walking out, speaking up, or getting help.

The traumatic events in our lives can keep us constrained, inhibiting our ability to move forward. Fear cripples our desire for more and challenges our worthiness. In order to leave the past, we must move forward.

God is not asking you to move forward alone. He wants to hold your hand and take every step with you. Don't be afraid of the waters. He wants you to move with Him.

Have you ever seen a waltz? The man takes the lead and the woman follows as they gracefully glide across the floor. God is going to make the journey from victim to victor with you. When you take His hand, He places His arm around your back and you'll glide forward as you rest, allowing Him to lead the way.

God makes this possible through the Holy Spirit, who empowers you to step into freedom. In taking the first step, you can rest as He assures you, "Everything will be fine."

God knows you're afraid. He knows your heart and is aware of all you've been through. He doesn't pressure you. He wants you to take your time, but, most importantly, He wants you to know that He's taking every step with you and empowering you along the way. The knowledge of God's presence is the factor that changes everything. In times of fear and insecurity in the Bible, you'll often find God directing the focus back to Himself. When you become aware that the Lord of Hosts is with you, it has a way of ushering you into a place of rest and assurance.

Moses didn't have super powers; he wasn't a hero or anyone special. He was just a person who found rest in God's presence, which enabled him to move forward. That same presence is with you today, giving you rest and empowering you to move on to better days.

PRAYER

Father, sometimes moving forward can seem scary because I don't know what lies ahead. But I must remember You are with me and I can find confidence in Your presence. It is in acknowledging Your presence that I can rest. I know that I can't move forward without first letting go of the past, so help me to release all that that is hindering me from moving on. In Jesus' name I pray, amen.

Personal Declaration

I am not bound by fear; I am moving forward with God.

Take Soul Care Actions

1. Is there a secret that you have been holding on to in fear? Share it here and release it to God once and for all.

   _____

   _____

   _____

2. What beliefs and habits do you want to keep, release, and establish today?

- Keep: _____

- Release: _____

- Establish: _____

Date:

TIME FOR
SELF-REFLECTION:

_____

_____

_____

_____

_____

_____

_____

_____

_____

_____

_____

_____

_____

_____

_____

_____

_____

_____

_____

Day 4

Trust in the Lord

Key Verse

You, LORD, give true peace to those who depend on you, because they trust you.

(Isaiah 26:3 NCV)

Thoughts
on Today's Key Verse

When was the last time that you were able to fully trust someone without reservations or second-guessing their intentions?

When we first come into this world, in our innocence we trust everyone until we are given a reason not to. Then, as we experience hurt, trials, and tribulations, we begin to do the opposite, which is to trust only those who have proven themselves worthy. Some of us find that few people give us reasons to trust them.

As a result, we build a wall of protection around our hearts. The only thing wrong with that is, while it keeps the wrong people out, it may also keep the right people away. It's only when we begin to trust God that He can (and will) tear down the walls erected in fear and hurt, as we allow him to come in and rebuild the broken places.

When we trust Him and depend on Him, He gives us peace. It's in His peace that we can finally rest, knowing we've found someone we can fully trust. The great thing about the peace of God is that you can have it regardless of what's going on around you. The whole world could be crumbling, but when you trust God, His peace will give you the ability to rest despite the circumstances.

Begin to trust God, and as you do, you'll find His peace will meet you where you are.

Prayer

Father, I want to trust You, and I need Your peace so I can rest. Show me how to depend on You. I'm tired of not having peace of mind, and I know You're the only one who can give it to me. I will trust You in the best way I know how, and I thank You in advance for Your peace and rest. In Jesus' name I pray, amen.

Personal
Declaration

I can trust God.

Take Soul Care Actions

1. Are you having difficulty trusting God? Why?

   _____

   _____

   _____

   _____

2. What beliefs and habits do you want to keep, release, and establish today?

   - Keep: _____

   - Release: _____

   - Establish: _____

Date:

TIME FOR
SELF-REFLECTION:

_____

_____

_____

_____

_____

_____

_____

_____

_____

_____

_____

_____

_____

_____

_____

_____

_____

_____

_____

_____

_____

Day 5

DON'T WORRY

Key Verse

Don't worry about anything; instead pray about everything. Tell God what you need and thank him for all He has done. Then you will experience God's peace, which exceeds anything we understand. His peace will guard your hearts and minds as you live in Christ Jesus.

(Philippians 4:6–7 NLT)

Thoughts on Today's Key Verse

Have you ever prayed about something and yet continued to worry? If so, you're not alone. Worrying is a natural reaction, often happening without us thinking about it. But it doesn't have to be that way.

Worry is a result of lack of rest and not trusting that prayers have been answered. Or maybe you're not taking things to God in prayer at all. The peace of God will give rest to your mind and your heart when you make your needs known to Him in prayer.

What exactly is prayer, anyway?

Prayer is literally a conversation with your Father. It's your opportunity to be vulnerable before the One who knows your heart. There is no need for formalities like kneeling or speaking eloquently. Come to the still waters just as you are and lay your head on your Father's lap. Forget the rest of the world and talk to God the same way you would your best friend.

It's okay to talk with Him by the waters. Prayer is like planting a seed. When we plant a seed, it's placed in the ground and watered. Then nature does its part to bring that seed to fruition. In the same way, when we share our needs with God through prayer, we're entrusting Him with our seed. Then just like nature, God makes sure our need is met.

The only thing left for us to do is thank Him, trusting that He has done his part. Don't allow worry to bring you into unrest when God is waiting to meet your needs.

The peace that God gives is something we can't comprehend with our natural minds. It's a peace that causes rest in situations where peace isn't normally found. People around you who know what you're going through will wonder how you're able to rest, and you'll gladly tell them why. Take your needs to the still waters, and exchange them for the peace that gives rest to your heart and mind as your prayers are answered by your loving Father.

PRAYER

Lord, I often find myself worrying about what I need or how things in my life will turn out. I now know my worry is a result of not giving my needs to You in prayer, and trusting that You will meet them. I surrender my worry to You today as I make my needs known. I receive Your peace that ushers me into true rest. In Jesus' name, amen.

Personal
Declaration

I can take all my needs to God in prayer.

Take Soul Care Actions

1. What have you been worrying about that you need to take to God in prayer?

   _____

   _____

   _____

2. What beliefs and habits do you want to keep, release, and establish today?

- Keep: _____

- Release: _____

- Establish: _____

Date:

TIME FOR
SELF-REFLECTION:

Day 6

WHERE SALVATION IS FOUND

Key Verse

I find rest in God; only He can save me. He is my rock and my salvation. He is my defender; I will not be defeated.

(Psalm 62:1–2 NCV)

Thoughts
on Today's Key Verse

Would you go to a car lot to find a house, or to a shoe store to get your hair done? The answer, of course, is no. But this is exactly what I was doing, and what many women find themselves doing, unwittingly. Sisters, we have all found ourselves seeking in the wrong place at one time or another.

Salvation can only be found in God. But like many, I was trying to find it in men. I wanted someone to deliver me from my past hurts and difficulties, someone to give me the love my heart was so desperate to find. What I really needed was a true Savior. At first it would seem I had found salvation, but what men could give me was only temporary. It was a surface-level salvation decoy that played off my emotions and had no ability to provide salvation for my soul.

As children, too, we often look to our parents to be our salvation, to save us from all our mistakes and bad decisions. But there is only One who can save, and that is God.

We can find rest in the fact that the salvation of God is an everlasting promise. His saving grace is an indwelling power that saves us not only from the hurts caused by others, but also from our reckless actions.

Be sure that, in your striving to escape the harsh realities of life, you're seeking salvation in the right place.

Prayer

Father, I have been looking for others to give me what only You can provide. Salvation comes from You alone, and there's no area of my life that cannot be saved when I turn to You. I can rest in Your salvation because You're not like man. I know I can depend on You, for You are my rock and my defender. In Jesus' name I pray, amen.

Personal
Declaration

I can rest knowing God is my salvation.

Take Soul Care Actions

1. In what other places have you been looking for salvation?

   _____

   _____

   _____

2. What beliefs and habits do you want to keep, release, and establish today?

- Keep: _____

- Release: _____

- Establish: _____

Date:

TIME FOR
SELF-REFLECTION:

_____

_____

_____

_____

_____

_____

_____

_____

_____

_____

_____

_____

_____

_____

_____

_____

_____

_____

DAY 7

FOCUSING ON GOD'S GOODNESS

KEY VERSE

I said to myself, "Relax and rest. God has showered you with blessings. Soul, you've been rescued from death; Eye, you've been rescued from tears; And you, Foot, were kept from stumbling."

(Psalm 116:7–8 MSG)

THOUGHTS ON TODAY'S KEY VERSE

Here we are at Day Seven. Hopefully, you've accepted God's invitation to come, learned to trust Him more, given Him your burdens, shared your secrets, and found rest.

Allow today to be a day of focus, where you intentionally concentrate on the good things God has done in your life. Even if you're unable to think of anything, think on what you would like Him to do. If you've felt yourself becoming overwhelmed with life, what you need may be a shift in focus. We can always find the blessings of God in our life if we look for them. We can also find the bad in life if we look for it. Neither is far away nor hard to discover; it's all a matter of what we choose to meditate on.

David, the writer of this psalm, could have easily focused on things that were going wrong in his life; instead he shifted his attention to how good God is. He was able to find rest in the goodness of God.

It's okay to focus on the water. You can listen to the rustling of the trees in the background or remain in the peace of the still waters. No matter how bad things have gotten in your life, the very breath in your body means it isn't over. You can do this! I know people have said otherwise; but take it from someone who's walked in your shoes: You. Can. Do. This.

Say it, believe it, and embrace it. Say it with me: "I. Have. Found. Rest!" God loves you, and He is a good God. When you choose to focus on His goodness, all else begins to fade away.

When the world seems to be closing in on you, it can be intimidating, but there's nothing more powerful than the One within you. Decide to seek Him in all you do, and don't be held back by life any longer. You've let things, people, and circumstances divert your attention for too long. It's time to bring your focus back to God.

Get rid of the distractions once and for all, and rest in the goodness of God.

PRAYER

Father, I must admit that it's easy to focus on all the negative things that are taking place in my life. But I now understand that focusing on Your goodness is a choice I make, regardless of my circumstances. Lord, help me to always choose to keep my focus on You. In Jesus' name, amen.

PERSONAL DECLARATION

I am focused on God's goodness.

TAKE SOUL CARE ACTIONS

1. What are two amazing things God has done in your life?

    _____

    _____

    _____

2. What beliefs and habits do you want to keep, release,
    and establish today?

*   Keep: _____

*   Release: _____

*   Establish: _____

Date:

Time for
Self-Reflection:

_____

_____

_____

_____

_____

_____

_____

_____

_____

_____

_____

_____

_____

_____

_____

_____

_____

_____

_____

_____

WEEK 2

ENJOY
REFRESHMENT

*"God has gifted you diverse experiences knit-
ted together with grace and beautifully displayed
in the design of your destiny."*

Leonie H. Mattison

DAY 8

GOD CARES ABOUT YOU

KEY VERSE

"I will refresh the weary and satisfy the faint."

(Jeremiah 31:25 NIV)

THOUGHTS
ON TODAY'S KEY VERSE

Jesus is concerned about our well-being, and our ability to push forward with purpose.

Once there was a group of people who had been following Jesus for three days. He pulled His disciples to the side out of concern because the multitude had not eaten anything. They didn't have the money or resources to provide for the vast crowd, but a little boy there had five loaves of bread and two fish. To the natural eye that wasn't enough food, but Jesus blessed it and instructed the disciples to distribute it to the multitude. In a matter of minutes, what had been a child's lunch became enough to feed over five thousand people—with leftovers!

Jesus could have easily sent the crowd home hungry to get their own food. But He saw they were weary and faint, and it's not the nature of God to leave us in that condition. The only thing the world can ever offer is a child's lunch, which will never be enough to sustain us. But when we come to God with what we have, He fills us.

Weariness is sometimes necessary, because it's in our state of emptiness that we seek to be filled. It's only in seeking that we find what we're looking for. We must choose to drink from the water source that never runs dry. God won't force us to come into His refreshment. It's okay to taste the water.

Many of us are waiting on God to make the first move. But He already has. He created you, loved you, and called you. It's now your turn to drink. We're refreshed in every area of our lives, receiving the needed confidence in His ever-present, always-faithful love for us. The journey can be tiring, and you may even want to give up at times; but that's when you allow the refreshing power of God to satisfy your dry places.

Immerse yourself in the waters of His presence, knowing, accepting, allowing, embracing, appreciating, and receiving the manifested, satisfying unconditional love of God that envelopes the threads of your life. Be in awe of His amazing flow of love empowering you to design a better life experience.

PRAYER

Lord, You know better than anyone how weary and tired I have grown on this journey. I thought my feeling of weariness was a part of life, so I accepted it. But I now know better. Thank You for caring about me and not leaving me to thirst alone. I surrender myself to Your refreshment, allowing my weariness to lift off under the power of Your love for me. In Jesus' name, amen.

Personal
Declaration

I am loved by God.

Take Soul Care Actions

1. What has been the cause of your weariness?

   _____

   _____

   _____

2. What beliefs and habits do you want to keep, release, and establish today?

   • Keep: _____

   • Release: _____

   • Establish: _____

Date:

TIME FOR
SELF-REFLECTION:

_____

_____

_____

_____

_____

_____

_____

_____

_____

_____

_____

_____

_____

_____

_____

_____

_____

_____

DAY 9

FOLLOW GOD'S PATH

KEY VERSE

He refreshes my soul. He guides me along the right paths for his name's sake.

(Psalm 23:3 NIV)

THOUGHTS
ON TODAY'S KEY VERSE

I thought I had a lover, but he turned out to be a luster. I thought I had a provider, but he turned out to be a user. I thought I had someone who cared about me, but I ended up being physically abused. I kept running into the arms of men who failed me. I thought my career would give me status and meaning, but instead I experienced bullying and harassment. I made God out of men and gave them my body and encountered pain and agony. I thought I needed intellectual stimulation but got corrupted with immorality.

I knew about Jesus, but I didn't know how to drink from Him. For years I wore a mask to hide the fact that I was empty, broken, and thirsty. My thirst was painful, a reminder that something in my heart was lacking, something in my soul was dry and empty. It was a wanting, a needing, a longing for what I was made of, whom I was made for, and why I was created.

I went down many wrong roads in search of purpose and self, but none of them ever led to the right destination—until I finally allowed God to lead me down the right path. My heart was thirsty for love, and I drank from many cups but it was never enough. Nothing I drank could ever quench the thirst.

It's okay to drink from the water until you're filled. It was at the still waters that I was finally filled. My thirst was quenched and my search for love was over. We can keep trying to fill ourselves with men and temporary fixes, but they'll never be enough.

Stop your search and put all your efforts into seeking God's path for you. His path for your life is a dependable one. It may not be as predictable as you want it to be, because it requires faith, but it will always be worth it.

You will always find refreshment where God leads. His is a path that can be trusted and was mapped out for you before the beginning of time. The power of the Holy Spirit dwells within you, acting as your personal GPS, guiding you in paths of righteousness for His name's sake.

No matter how far you've veered off course, God will reroute you and set you back on track. Today, forsake your own way and seek the path that leads to the manifestation of His perfect will for you.

PRAYER

Father in heaven, I have gone down my own path before and trusted my own ways. You know where that has gotten me. I want Your path, I want Your ways, I want Your refreshment. I don't know how far I am from the path You've called me to walk on. But I know You're the only one who can get me there, and I'm trusting You to do just that. So I release the wheel to my life to You. I give You permission to take over control and get me where You have called me to be. In Jesus' name, amen.

PERSONAL DECLARATION

God is guiding me on the right path.

TAKE SOUL CARE ACTIONS

1. What are some ways you can stay on God's path?

    _____

    _____

    _____

2. What beliefs and habits do you want to keep, release,
    and establish today?

    *   Keep: _____

    *   Release: _____

    *   Establish: _____

Date:

TIME FOR SELF-REFLECTION:

_____

_____

_____

_____

_____

_____

_____

_____

_____

_____

_____

_____

_____

_____

_____

_____

DAY 10

LET GOD TAKE CARE OF YOU

KEY VERSE

So repent [change your inner self, your old way of thinking, regret past sins] and return [to God; seek His purpose for your life], so that your sins may be wiped away [blotted out, completely erased], so that times of refreshing may come from the presence of the Lord [restoring you like a cool wind on a hot day].

(Acts 3:19 AMP)

THOUGHTS
ON TODAY'S KEY VERSE

I remember as a kid being outside, playing all day under the sweltering sun. Coming in from outside was always bittersweet because, as much as I wanted to continue playing, there was nothing like stepping into the cool air and taking my first sip of ice-cold water.

You've been deprived of life-giving water for too long. Your soul has been dry and empty, needing the refreshing touch of the Holy Spirit. Your old sins and past ways will plague you no more, and although your journey has been exhausting, you will find all the strength you need by the water.

God doesn't want you to just stop when you have taken the first sip. He wants to be sure you are fully refreshed. It's okay to be refreshed by the water.

The refreshment of the Lord revitalizes your soul and gives you a new sense of purpose. The world will suck you dry and leave you feeling as though you have nothing left to offer. But when you drink from the still waters, you'll be filled with purpose. When you're beside the still waters, you're acknowledged. You're catered to, seen, heard, and fully cared for.

Despite what you may think or what others may say, there is no mistake, no bad decision too big or small for your Father to wash away. It's only once your sins are gone that you can sit beside the still waters in the presence of God and receive the refreshment you need.

Prayer

Lord, I have allowed life to suck me dry, and circumstances have gotten the best of me. I want to be refreshed as You erase all that tries to tie me to a past that can't have me. Forgive me, Father, for what I have done, for the mistakes and bad decisions I have made. Thank You for erasing that part of my life. I receive your refreshment as I dwell in your presence. In Jesus' name, amen.

PERSONAL DECLARATION

My sins are wiped away and I am refreshed in the presence of God.

TAKE SOUL CARE ACTIONS

1. What are some things that have been sucking your life dry?

   _____

   _____

   _____

2. What beliefs and habits do you want to keep, release, and establish today?

   - Keep: _____

   - Release: _____

   - Establish: _____

Date:

TIME FOR
SELF-REFLECTION:

_____

_____

_____

_____

_____

_____

_____

_____

_____

_____

_____

_____

_____

_____

_____

_____

_____

_____

_____

DAY 11

THE TRUTH
SETS YOU FREE

KEY VERSE

The law of the LORD is perfect, refreshing the soul.

(Psalm 19:7 NIV)

Thoughts on Today's Key Verse

"In the beginning was the Word, and the Word was with God, and the Word was God" (John 1:1 NIV). Allow the Holy Spirit to awaken Himself within you, causing stillness to rule.

When I first started to read my Bible, I thought it was filled with a bunch of laws that had to be kept for God to love me. Boy, was I wrong! I still know people who think this way, but it's because they're unable to see the love in the letter.

When the Scripture uses the word law, it's simply talking about instructions from the Bible. Depending on one's experience in their life with "the law," the word can sometimes have a negative connotation. However, the Word of God is His love for us in providing us with direction and boundaries. In them we can find protection and refreshment for our soul.

Just as our phones come with manuals to make sure we're operating them properly, so, too, is the Bible our manual for life. Sometimes your phone gets crowded with too much junk or is just not functioning as it should, and you have the option to do a reset. When you reset the device, it returns to its original settings.

When we read the Word of God, we're pressing the reset button for our lives. The world can cause you to forget who you really are or what God has said about you, but when you read the Word, it refreshes your memory. It is okay to trust the reflection on the waters.

Today, be reminded that the Word of God comes to quiet your heart, reset your mind, refresh your soul, and fuel your faith. Open the Word and allow it to subdue the noise of the mind and up-root every hindrance to your peace. No matter what you've been through, it's never too late to let the refreshing Word of God reset you to whom God has created you to be. It's easy to lose sight of your identity, but if you have the refreshing power of God's Word, you're never far from your true self.

There are many self-help and motivational books that will leave you feeling good and charged up but have no true transformation-al power. Only the Bible has the ability to transform. Spend some time reading the Word of God, and allow it to refresh your soul. Let it remind you who you are: a Daughter of the Most High God.

Soon after, you'll be able to rise, take control of your life, and become the woman who allows the personal power within to re-lease the pain from her yesterday, and thread the peace of God into today.

PRAYER

I admit, Lord, that I have taken on an identity that has been the result of the terrible things that have happened in my life. But I know that's not who I am. Help me to turn to Your Word when I find myself lost, and allow it to refresh my memory of who I am in You. May it wash away every false sense of self that has haunted me over the years. Thank You for Your Word and its transformational power. Today, I choose to press the reset button on my life. In Jesus' name, amen. .

PERSONAL
DECLARATION

I am refreshed by the Word of God.

TAKE SOUL CARE ACTIONS

1. What time will you set aside to read the Word of God?

   _____

   _____

   _____

2. What beliefs and habits do you want to keep, release,
   and establish today?

   • Keep: _____

   • Release: _____

   • Establish: _____

Date:

TIME FOR
SELF-REFLECTION:

_____

_____

_____

_____

_____

_____

_____

_____

_____

_____

_____

_____

_____

_____

_____

_____

_____

_____

DAY 12

GOD
IS MOVING

KEY VERSE

"Forget about what's happened; don't keep going over old history. Be alert, be present. I'm about to do something brand-new. It's bursting out! Don't you see it? There it is! I'm making a road through the desert, rivers in the badlands. Wild animals will say 'Thank you!'—the coyotes and the buzzards—because I provided water in the desert, rivers through the sunbaked earth, drinking water for the people I chose, the people I made especially for myself, a people custom-made to praise me."

(Isaiah 43:16–21 MSG)

THOUGHTS ON TODAY'S KEY VERSE

God is moving, not stuck in the past. He's making new inroads, forging ahead.

It's the things we've gone through in our past that have depleted us of our resources to be victorious in life. Although you may still feel the sting of pain, when you allow the still waters of refreshing to wash over you, your past becomes separated from you. God is doing something new in your life, but it doesn't exist in the past and that's why you can't stay there.

Every time we travel to the past, we're subjecting ourselves to the same emptiness we experienced at that time. You're human and sometimes the past will try to remind you of who you were, but the refreshing presence of God will remind you of who you are. It's okay to bathe in the water.

Have you ever been to an event where they were serving refreshments? Crackers and cheese, fruit and finger foods and the like. They're usually something light, just enough to snack on but not enough to fill you. It's the equivalent of being thirsty and someone giving you a cup of water.

That's not the type of refreshment God has for you. His cup of refreshment never runs dry. It's a continuous flow of vital life and energy—a washing over that keeps you free of the past so you can walk into the new things He is doing in your life.

Sisters, God is moving! He's filling the dryness with the refreshing waters of life in places that your past has declared dead.

Prayer

Lord, many hurtful things have taken place in my past, and I know I've allowed them to affect me for too long. Whether I can see it now or not, I know that You're doing a new thing in my life. Father, wash over me with your never-ending waters of refreshment. Keep me clean and free of the past so I may come into all that You have planned for me. In Jesus' name, amen.

Personal
Declaration

I am not my past.

Take Soul Care Actions

1. What about the past do you need to let go of?

   _____

   _____

   _____

2. What beliefs and habits do you want to keep, release, and establish today?

   • Keep: _____

   • Release: _____

   • Establish: _____

Date:

TIME FOR
SELF-REFLECTION:

_____

_____

_____

_____

_____

_____

_____

_____

_____

_____

_____

_____

_____

_____

_____

_____

_____

_____

_____

DAY 13

WISDOM FROM ON HIGH

KEY VERSE

Don't think for a moment that you know it all, for wisdom comes when you adore Him with undivided devotion and avoid everything that's wrong. Then you will find the healing refreshment your body and spirit long for.

(Proverbs 3:7–8 TPT)

Thoughts
on Today's Key Verse

Have you ever gone in search of answers, only to come back empty-handed? I have, and it can leave you feeling helpless. As women, we can often be independent to a fault. In our stubbornness, and even in the attempt to avoid hurt, we try to figure it all out on our own. We think we have all the answers, which sometimes leaves us in worse circumstances.

Everything we need dwells within the still waters of the Holy Spirit's wisdom. But it can be easy to get off course. When life throws things at us, we can get so anxious for answers and solutions that we come up with them on our own, believing we know what's right. Sometimes we act, knowing we have no clue as to what to do; we just know we must do something.

It's okay to seek His wisdom at the water. There's only one thing you must do. Quiet yourself and allow the Spirit of God to speak the wisdom that you need for whatever you're going through. The wisdom of God is like releasing a reservoir of water in a dry desert. It brings refreshment and life to everything in its path.

When walking away from a life full of trauma and pain, you may have to make some tough decisions. Those decisions are not meant to be made alone. Allow God to refresh and pour into you His divine wisdom for your situation.

Today, awaken to the repetitions of God through His Word, reminding us to reconnect to the fullness of His amazing flow of inspiration, strength, wisdom and insight. Allow the still waters to run over your mind, to refresh and ease your thoughts so that you can think clearly and discern the wisdom of the Father.

Prayer

Lord, it seems there's always a decision that needs to be made, and I now know that I don't need to make them without You. Father, help me to find refreshment in Your wisdom, and release me of my need to find all the answers on my own. In Jesus' name, amen.

Personal Declaration

I am refreshed by God's wisdom.

Take Soul Care Actions

1. In what areas of your life do you need God's wisdom?

   _____

   _____

   _____

2. What beliefs and habits do you want to keep, release, and establish today?

   • Keep: _____

   • Release: _____

   • Establish: _____

Date:

TIME FOR
SELF-REFLECTION:

_____

_____

_____

_____

_____

_____

_____

_____

_____

_____

_____

_____

_____

_____

_____

_____

_____

_____

_____

_____

DAY 14

REFRESHMENT OVERFLOWS

KEY VERSE

You're all I want in heaven! You're all I want on earth! When my skin sags and my bones get brittle, GOD is rock-firm and faithful. Look! Those who left you are falling apart! Deserters, they'll never be heard from again. But I'm in the very presence of GOD—oh, how refreshing it is! I've made Lord GOD my home. GOD, I'm telling the world what you do!

(Psalm 73:25–28 MSG)

Thoughts
on Today's Key Verse

I think we all remember what our lives were like without God. Personally, I can say that I was nothing without Him. God has been and still is everything that He has promised in His Word, and when we allow ourselves to find refreshment in the still waters, we allow Him to be just that.

Refreshment is found in the presence of God. There is never lack when in the presence of the Father. The refreshment found by the still waters is not meant to be kept there. It's meant to be shared with others. First we fill ourselves, and then we allow the Holy Spirit to overflow into the lives of others through us. It's okay to share the water with others.

Once you're refreshed, you can lead others to the still waters you've found. God wants to use you and everything you've been through to reach others. He takes what was painful and uses it to bring healing to other souls. God doesn't waste your heartache; He recycles it and turns it into something that someone else needs. We are nothing without God, but with Him we are an unstoppable force.

Someone who's completely depleted of life and energy is re- vived once they've been refreshed. I hope that you've found the dry places in your life being revived as you drink from the still waters.

Don't let this be the last time. May you be continually refreshed so that you can be continually refreshing to those around you. Bless others with your words. Offer sweet, kind words that uplift and encourage. Remember, that's who you are! Don't change who you are because of negative circumstances. Remain in the truth of your God-given identity and continual refreshment.

What is good is becoming better and brighter every day.

Prayer

Father, I know that without You I'm nothing, and I'm glad that I never have to live another day without being in Your presence. Help me to continually find my refreshment in You. Thank You, for although my past was full of hurt, You have cleansed me of it and taken it and turned it into something to help others. Whenever I am feeling drained and empty, help me find my way back to the still waters. In Jesus' name, amen.

Personal Declaration

I am refreshed to refresh others.

Take Soul Care Actions

1. Whom do you know who could benefit from the refreshment of the still waters?

   _____

   _____

   _____

2. What beliefs and habits do you want to keep, release, and establish today?

   • Keep: _____

   • Release: _____

   • Establish: _____

Date:

Time for
Self-Reflection:

_____

_____

_____

_____

_____

_____

_____

_____

_____

_____

_____

_____

_____

_____

_____

_____

_____

WEEK 3

RECEIVE RESTORATION

"All people have multi-colored, multi-purpose threads of their unique experiences woven into the beautiful design of their destiny. Each thread has been formed by a trial experienced and conquered, a truth told, a potential unlocked, or a purpose accomplished. How you weave these threads together will determine the masterpiece you create."

Leonie H. Mattison

Day 15

ENCOURAGE EACH OTHER DAILY

KEY VERSE

Finally, my brothers and sisters, rejoice! Strive for full resto-
ration, encourage one another, be of one mind, live in peace.
And the God of love and peace will be with you.

(2 Corinthians 13:11 NIV)

THOUGHTS ON TODAY'S KEY VERSE

My sister, now is a time of celebration. Rejoice, for your past is brought to nothing as your future comes to life in the light of Christ's love for you. **Don't just allow God to restore some areas; allow Him to restore them all.** Scripture tells us to strive for full restoration.

If you think about the word strive, it means to press on. Restoration is more than taking a seat and sticking your toes in the water; it means pressing forward into the deep parts of the water. It means getting dirt between your toes as you stand firmly on the ground of God's Word.

It's okay to go to the deep part of the waters. Many fail in this place because they strive for full restoration all alone. I understand that trusting others is hard, and that you've been hurt by those you trusted. But this time things will be different.

Put your trust in the Holy Spirit, and allow Him to guide you to those who will encourage you. When you lean on your own understanding, you can end up on a road you never intended; but when you trust and obey the leading of the Holy Spirit, there's no way you'll go wrong.

Sometimes you may not want to strive; you may even want to give up. That's when having fellowship with other believers comes into play. We must encourage one another so that we can keep pressing toward the mark of full restoration.

Restoring a house may mean knocking some walls down, or even pulling out some appliances. But all of this is done so something better can be created. When people see the new house, they'll have no idea of its dilapidated condition before.

That's exactly what God wants to do with your life, if you'll allow Him to. Press into Him so you can be fully restored, lacking nothing. Allow the Holy Spirit to guide you to others who will keep you uplifted along the way.

PRAYER

Father, I don't want to be restored in only some areas. I don't want any stone left unturned. I want to be restored to the person You created me to be. I want to be the person You see when You look at me. I know it will take work and it won't be easy. Father, I ask that You lead me to people who will encourage and uplift me—people who have a heart like Yours, whose desire is to do me no harm but to bring me closer to You. Thank you for the restoring power of your Holy Spirit. In Jesus' name, amen.

PERSONAL
DECLARATION

I am restored in all areas of my life.

TAKE SOUL CARE ACTIONS

1. In what areas of your life do you need restoration?

   _____

   _____

   _____

2. What beliefs and habits do you want to keep, release, and establish today?

- Keep: _____

- Release: _____

- Establish: _____

Date:

TIME FOR
SELF-REFLECTION:

_____

_____

_____

_____

_____

_____

_____

_____

_____

_____

_____

_____

_____

_____

_____

_____

_____

_____

DAY 16

THE JOY
OF
THE LORD

KEY VERSE

Restore to me the joy of your salvation and grant me a willing spirit, to sustain me.

(Psalm 51:12 NIV)

THOUGHTS ON TODAY'S KEY VERSE

Your life is busy. A lot of people are depending on you to get things done, and if you don't, who else will? Stop! Clear your mind for a few moments. Don't think about the list of things you need to do—who needs what, or even what you're going to eat for lunch. Just think about the saving grace of our Lord Jesus Christ, and the tremendous love God must have for you to sentence Him to death on your behalf.

Consider the beating He endured, the lashes on His back, and the skin hanging from His bones, which made Him unrecognizable. The Bible says there was no beauty found in Him (Isaiah 53:2). He was full of sorrow, and as much as He may have wanted to pass up the cup of suffering and death, He knew He had to endure because of God's love for us. So He did. He endured the persecution, the shame, the beating, being spat on and hung to die as a criminal. A man sinless, blameless, and stripped of glory all so we could walk in freedom and complete restoration of all that God intended for us.

It's okay to bask in the joy of the waters. Think about every time God has come through for you, times that you didn't even deserve. How can you think on those things and not rejoice? That's the joy He wants you to walk in, to remain in. David prayed for a willing spirit to sustain him, but we now have the Holy Spirit.

Being restored to the joy of God's saving grace means walking in constant understanding of all He has done for you and how much He loves you. It means **allowing the calming waters of the Holy Spirit to remind you of God's saving grace.** Life gets difficult, and it's not hard to forget that you must choose to walk in His grace. Remember that the same grace that delivered and restored you yesterday is the same grace that will restore you today.

Be restored in joy as you meditate on the salvation of God.

Prayer

Lord, happiness is fleeting and can come and go, depending on what is taking place in my life. I want more than tempo-rary spouts of happiness. I know that the joy I receive from You is something that no man can take from me—a joy that is found in Christ. It remains with me, even in the darkest of hours. Father, restore joy in me, a joy that I have never known before. In Jesus' name, amen.

PERSONAL DECLARATION

I have the joy of the Lord.

TAKE SOUL CARE ACTIONS

1. Describe some times when God came through for you.

   _____

   _____

   _____

2. What beliefs and habits do you want to keep, release, and establish today?

   • Keep: _____

   • Release: _____

   • Establish: _____

Date:

TIME FOR
SELF-REFLECTION:

_____

_____

_____

_____

_____

_____

_____

_____

_____

_____

_____

_____

_____

_____

_____

_____

_____

_____

_____

DAY 17

A GOD
OF HIS WORD

KEY VERSE

*Heal me, LORD, and I will be healed; save me and I will be
saved, for you are the one I praise.*

(Jeremiah 17:14 NIV)

Thoughts
on Today's Key Verse

One of the reasons I love this Scripture is because, when God does something, it is done! Have you ever had someone say they would do something, but then did a halfway job or didn't do what you asked at all? They come back with some type of excuse, trying to explain why they weren't able to do what they said. God, unlike man, does not give excuses. If He said something, it'll be done—no ifs, ands, or buts about it. God is a God of His word, and He has been since the beginning of time. His Word is the only word that can be fully trusted and relied upon.

It's okay to be sure of the water. When you come to God seeking restoration, expect just that. God said that He wouldn't give us a stone for bread (Matthew 7:9–11). In other words, even if He doesn't give you exactly what you ask for, you can trust that He has something better in mind.

While you're in the waters, it may not feel like anything. It may not seem like much is happening. But, if you continue to submit yourself to God, you'll see areas of your life that are being changed: lost finances that are replenished, destroyed relationships that are rebuilt, loss of self-confidence that is found.

We sometimes underestimate the power of what God can do in our life, and we hinder our receiving when we do that. Don't think for a second that anything is too big for God. Even if it's healing for your body. Perhaps you've been through things that have had a negative effect on your body, whether it be a disease, the results of physical abuse or sickness, or stress–induced symptoms.

"Heal me, LORD, and I will be healed." Do you believe it? Dare to believe that God is exactly who He says He is and will do exactly what He said He would. That's when you'll see true restoration in your life as never before. **Get out of your own way and allow God to be God.** He has been the Father for a long time, and He knows what He's doing. When He says He'll restore you, that's what He means. Allow Him to do it.

PRAYER

People sometimes do things halfway, but not You, God. Help me to take the limits off You and know that there's no area of my life that's too complicated to experience Your restoration. Many people don't keep their word, but, Father, help me to see that You do—always. You're faithful to Your word, and forever will be. In Jesus' name, amen.

Personal
Declaration

I am the child of a God who always sticks to His word.

Take Soul Care Actions

1. What are some ways you can live life with expectancy?

   _____

   _____

   _____

2. What beliefs and habits do you want to keep, release,
   and establish today?

- Keep: _____

- Release: _____

- Establish: _____

Date:

TIME FOR
SELF-REFLECTION:

_____

_____

_____

_____

_____

_____

_____

_____

_____

_____

_____

_____

_____

_____

_____

_____

_____

DAY 18

GOD HAS A PLAN FOR YOU

KEY VERSE

"For I know the plans I have for you," declares the Lord, "plans to prosper you and not harm you, plans to give you a hope and a future."

(Jeremiah 29:11 NIV)

Thoughts
on Today's Key Verse

I don't know about you, but I think it's such good news that God has a plan for each of us! I haven't always been sure about the direction of my life — but He has. He knows every turn, every stop, every detour, and, more importantly, how to get me to where He has called me to be.

Many people get concerned with whether they're in the will of God or if past mistakes and circumstances have taken them off course. I have news for you: **Google Maps has nothing on God.** He will restore you and put you right where you're supposed to be. He has a blueprint for your life, and just like Google Maps, He knows how to reroute you when you get off course.

You see, when you trust God for the direction of your life, His plan will come to pass for you. Despite what you may believe or even how things may seem, you're not alone in the world trying to find your own way. You can be if you choose to, but we've all been there before and that road leads to a dead-end.

It's okay to forsake your path and walk in the waters. Ditch the familiar road with all the stops you've already taken. Give God control of your life so He can restore you back to the plan He created. You're never too far away. God has no plans to harm you as others have. His plans are only good for you. His desire is to see you prosper, and His plan for you gives you a hope and a future that's brighter than the sun itself.

So don't fret. Don't worry about mess-ups and falls in the plan of God. Just know that, when you surrender yourself at the still waters, when you surrender you own will and ask that His will be done instead, **God will restore you to the path that He has always had for your life.**

Prayer

Father, I have made plans of my own; some worked and others didn't. I don't know how far I am from the plans that You've made for my life, but I'm trusting that You'll restore me back to the blueprint that You designed just for me. I know that, if I'm in Your will, I can't go wrong. So, Father, I say not my will, but Your will be done. In Jesus' name, amen.

PERSONAL
DECLARATION

I am living God's plan for my life.

TAKE SOUL CARE ACTIONS

1. What plans for your life do you need to surrender to God?

    _____

    _____

    _____

2. What beliefs and habits do you want to keep, release,
    and establish today?

*   Keep: _____

*   Release: _____

*   Establish: _____

Date:

TIME FOR
SELF-REFLECTION:

_____

_____

_____

_____

_____

_____

_____

_____

_____

_____

_____

_____

_____

_____

_____

_____

_____

_____

DAY 19

GOD HEALS YOUR WOUNDS

KEY VERSE

"But I will restore you to health and heal your wounds,"
declares the Lord.

(Jeremiah 30:17 NIV)

THOUGHTS ON TODAY'S KEY VERSE

We've already talked about God's ability to heal our physical bodies. But let's talk about a different kind of wound. These wounds go deeper than the physical body: they penetrate our very soul. Grandmother's ointment is not able to heal these wounds; only coming to the still waters and allowing the Holy Spirit Himself to cover you will heal these wounds.

They come from trauma—physical, emotional, sexual, and/or spiritual abuse, which can't be covered up with a band-aid. Many women are wounded and remain wounded for the rest of their life, living in fear and insecurity, allowing the things of the past to cloud their present and future.

Beloved, all that stops here. God is the healer of your wounds. You may have wounds that are so deep and pushed down that you don't even realize they're still there. He will heal even those, if you let Him. He wants to restore you to complete health—and that means your soul.

It's okay to lie in the water. Slip in and lie back, allowing your entire body to be submerged. You see, you must give everything over to God in order to receive true restoration for your soul. He'll restore parts of you that have negatively been affecting your life, even ones that you have no idea about.

There's no wound that will be left to hurt you when God is finished. You may be reluctant to surrender everything to God because it may not feel good. It may mean facing things you never wanted to deal with again or even thinking about things that you never wanted to think about again. That's okay. You can trust the Holy Spirit, and you can trust that God is going to restore all those areas of hurt and trauma back to health and wholeness.

Prayer

Give You everything, Lord? That sounds a little scary, if I'm honest, because I've never given those dark places to anyone before. But I know that, if I don't give them to You, You can't heal them. So I make that choice of faith today. Father, I surrender. I give You every wound, every hurt, everything that has happened to me that still haunts me, and every fear that is affecting my present life. I receive Your healing power and ability to restore my soul to complete health. In Jesus' name, amen.

PERSONAL DECLARATION

I am no longer wounded; I am restored.

TAKE SOUL CARE ACTIONS

1. What wounds are you releasing to God for complete healing?

   _____

   _____

   _____

2. What beliefs and habits do you want to keep, release, and establish today?

- Keep: _____

- Release: _____

- Establish: _____

Date:

TIME FOR
SELF-REFLECTION:

_____

_____

_____

_____

_____

_____

_____

_____

_____

_____

_____

_____

_____

_____

_____

_____

_____

_____

_____

_____

_____

_____

_____

_____

_____

_____

_____

_____

_____

_____

_____

_____

_____

_____

_____

_____

_____

_____

_____

DAY 20

EXPECT GOD'S BEST

KEY VERSE

Instead of your shame you will receive a double portion, and instead of disgrace you will rejoice in your inheritance. And so you will inherit a double portion in your land, and ever-lasting joy will be yours.

(Isaiah 61:7 NIV)

THOUGHTS ON TODAY'S KEY VERSE

The still waters is a place of both giving and receiving. We give God the things that have negatively been affecting us, and He gives us the restoration we need to move on to a new and better life in Him. Things have happened in your life that the Enemy intended for your harm. But God is taking those things, turning them into something beautiful, and using them for your good.

It's okay to leave everything at the waters and take all God has to give.

"You will inherit a double portion in your land." What is your land? Your land is your home, your job, your business, your children, your sphere of influence. **God's restoration blesses everything around you.** He can do more with your shame and disgrace than you've ever imagined. He will take the effects of wrong-doing and turn it into a business, a platform, a brand, and an opportunity to positively affect others' lives.

You must live a life of expectancy for God's restoration. You must know that He is restoring you, and you must expect to see the blessing of that restoration all over your life. If you tell me I'm going to the woods, I expect to see trees. If you tell me I'm going to the beach, I expect to see sand and sea. In the same way, God has promised you restoration and you can expect to see His blessing. So live in a place of expectation.

Joy is yours; it belongs to you. Your days of shame and disgrace are over. The Enemy may have formed a weapon against you, but that weapon can't be held against you when God is involved. God is restoring you; He is blessing you and caring for you. He is covering you with His double portion.

You have lived too long in a place of shame, and **God is calling you out to your place of victory and blessing.** You must walk in it, believe it, and expect it!

Prayer

Lord, I want to walk in Your blessing. I can see now that it's Your will for me to be blessed and that Your blessings are tied to Your restoration. I'm not used to living a life of expectation. My position was to expect the worst. But I now need to learn how to expect the best, how to expect Your restoration and blessing every day of my life. So I will take baby steps and start where I am, expecting Your goodness to be revealed. In Jesus' name, amen..

PERSONAL DECLARATION

I am restored; I am blessed.

TAKE SOUL CARE ACTIONS

1. What can you expect God to do in your life?

   _____

   _____

   _____

2. What beliefs and habits do you want to keep, release, and establish today?

- Keep: _____

- Release: _____

- Establish: _____

Date:

TIME FOR
SELF-REFLECTION:

_____

_____

_____

_____

_____

_____

_____

_____

_____

_____

_____

_____

_____

_____

_____

_____

_____

_____

_____

DAY 21

THE GOD
OF
COMPASSION

KEY VERSE

Then the Lord your God will rescue you from your captivity! He will have mercy upon you and come and gather you out of all the nations where he will have scattered you.

(Deuteronomy 30:3 TLB)

THOUGHTS ON TODAY'S KEY VERSE

Captivity. It sounds like such a harsh word and one that you may not be able to relate to. But we have all been in a place of captivity at some point in our lives. Some have been held captive by the opinions of others, while others have been held captive by their own hurt and shame. Then there's the big one: fear. Most people have been held captive by fear in some way at some time.

We've already learned that God will restore our soul and deal with all our wounds. Today we're going to think about compassion. God's compassion for you is more than you can probably wrap your head around. He cares so much about you that He calls you the apple of His eye.

Try to imagine the most compassionate person you can think of, the person who has shown you the most genuine love and care. You probably have a smile on your face just thinking about that person. Now imagine your Father God, who is infinitely more compassionate than that person.

God wants you to know that He loves and cares for you in a way that no one else can. His compassion is not out of pity; He doesn't feel sorry for you. The compassion that God has for you is solely out of His love and desire to see the greatness He has placed inside of you manifested in your life and the lives of those around you.

He has no interest in allowing you to live the way you did before. He loves you too much to leave you in that place. He wants to restore you and bring you into a new life with Him. **Allow the compassion of God to deliver you from captivity once and for all, providing complete restoration for your body and soul.**

Prayer

Father, there are areas in my life where I've been held captive, and I may still be captive to some things, but I'm here because I need You to set me free from all of them. I need Your loving compassion to restore my soul as I walk in the freedom You have provided for me through Christ. In Jesus' name I pray, amen.

Personal
Declaration

God loves me: I am free.

Take Soul Care Actions

1. On this last day of the devotional, write down what you've held back that you need to give to God.

   _____

   _____

   _____

2. What beliefs and habits do you want to keep, release, and establish today?

• Keep: _____

• Release: _____

• Establish: _____

Date:

TIME FOR
SELF-REFLECTION:

_____

_____

_____

_____

_____

_____

_____

_____

_____

_____

_____

_____

_____

_____

_____

_____

_____

_____

My Love for You Is Real

By LEONIE H MATTISON

You knitted me inside my mother's womb,
You have known me in and within the birth of time,
When I'm down, you lift my spirits high,
When I'm lost, you find me each time,
When I despair, you're my reason to smile,
I know I'm blessed without a doubt.

You alone hold the key to my heart,
The sensation of your presence makes me whole,
When I think of you, my heart leaps happily.
When you speak into my spirit lovingly,
I grow wings each time I listen to you,
Your words are enough to uplift me,
Making me feel like my soul is healed.

You are my dream come true—
Indescribable, unchangeable, available.
I know with you in my life I am forever satisfied,
With your might and grace,
I know I am free to live true happiness
and enjoy closeness with you.

I love you, God; you are the reason for my being!

MY STORY

LEONIE H. MATTISON

I'm Leonie, and I know from experience how important it is to trust and follow God when nothing else makes sense. Everything around you is yelling and you're in need of something—someone—to quiet the noise. I know. I understand.

I was a victim of emotional, sexual, and spiritual abuse, and have survived serious bouts of Bell's palsy and a stroke all before the age of thirty-six. None of those things caused me to be defeated. That victim became the victor who stands here today. I became more than just someone who survived. I became victorious.

It hasn't always been that way though. But the experience paid off. Having experienced assault throughout my life, relating to women who are hurting as a result of traumatic injuries comes easy to me. Like these women, life held me hostage to abuse at the hands of people who I thought cared about me. I was sexually abused at a young age, and manipulated into accepting sexual advances.

This abuse of power stripped me of my own personal power. I was left feeling hopeless and confused. Was I to blame for these assaults? Should I have made greater efforts to stop them? I now know that my mind was filled with lies stemming from my abusers. I now know that I was molested, like many other women, and that I was taken advantage of by those men.

They acted in sin and hurt a child, depriving me of my innocence. Until I sought help for my trauma, their selfish sexual desires caused me years of unhealthy behavior, self-doubt, and depression.

I knew I needed help to overcome my pain, but my trust was broken again and again. The resiliency I felt after the molestations and emotional abuse was ebbing, and I was unsure of how to go on. On one hand I felt used by men, but on the other I was confused about my role in the situation, unsure if I had given consent.

So, I did what many other women do: I kept silent. I had been taught to keep quiet. I lived in an environment where sharing my story would only lead to more pain and suffering, so I hid it. I tucked my trauma away, hiding it in my heart where no one would find it. I chose to internalize my pain and avoid the conflict.

Having been assaulted by so many authority figures in my life, I had no idea where to turn for help. I confided in women I looked up to, desperately seeking a safe place to unload the heavy burden. But those women were not true to their word, and, like a fallen vase of dead roses, my heart was broken yet again. Instead of being welcomed with open arms, I was greeted with scorn. Instead of seeing my need for help, they only compounded my shame.

I began to lose all hope for recovery. But even in my place of hiding, I was found by God. I reached out to Him in desperation, begging Him to send help, to show me a way out of my suffering. I had desperately wanted to feel the love of Christ through others. In my naïve search for healthy intimacy with others, I was left broken, battered, and torn.

Like a stone thrown in the sea, I sank deeper and deeper into depression with no one to pull me out. God was silent, so far away. I couldn't hear His voice or see an answer to my prayers. I was alone. I had nothing. No one left in the world. I attempted suicide.

Yet the life I longed to end was the very life God wanted to revive. Just like the still waters, His silence didn't mean He wasn't there. And in His love, I found the forgiveness and grace to renew my faith and bring healing to every broken part of me. In the process, I discovered what we all need to know: there is a personal power within each Christian that no one can take away—it's the Holy Spirit residing within every true believer. He protected me during my darkest hour and rekindled my hope for happiness.

Today I'm empowered to share my journey without shame or retribution. I didn't do it alone; I needed God's help. Along the way I discovered that, as a child of God, I have His Spirit within me, a personal Counselor who is always there, ready to comfort, guide, and protect me.

Through the Holy Spirit I learned how to rise and take control of my life. I used what He taught me to bridge the gap between pain and promise, and co-create with Jesus to design a better life.

My life story is much like a quilt of little scraps of fabric that, in themselves, appear useless—worthless, even. But when you put them all together, they become a beautiful covering that provides warmth and security. Each piece is unique, telling its own story.

Many of the scraps of your life may seem worthless, too. But when you allow God to sew them all together in love, they'll complete your story and give purpose to your pain.

I'm using my story to help women unlock their true potential and rise to the best version of themselves, all while giving praise to God, the Father of heaven and earth. My vision is to see women and girls survive and heal after abuse. I believe that through God's healing, grace, and redemption, all Christian women can survive—and even thrive—after an abuse.

APPENDIX:

BIBLE VERSES

1. "Come!" Anyone who is thirsty should come to Jesus. He will give the water of true life to anyone who wants it. They will not have to pay anything for it (Revelation 22:17 EASY).

2. "…those who drink the water I give will never be thirsty again. It becomes a fresh, bubbling spring within them, giving them eternal life" (John 4:14 NLT).

3. "He offers a resting place for me in his luxurious love. His tracks take me to an oasis of peace, the quiet brook of bliss. That's where he restores and revives my life. He opens before me pathways to God's pleasure and leads me along in his footsteps of righteousness so that I can bring honor to his name" (Psalms 23:2–3 TPT).

4. Delight yourself in the LORD, and he will give you the desires of your heart (Psalm 37:4 ESV).

5. "Come to me, all of you who are tired and have heavy loads, and I will give you rest. Accept my teachings and learn from me, because I am gentle and humble in spirit, and you will find rest for your lives. The burden that I ask you to accept is easy; the load I give you to carry is light" (Matthew 11:28–30 NCV).

6. Those who live in the shelter of the Most High will find rest in the shadow of the Almighty. This I declare about the LORD: He alone is my refuge, my place of safety; he is my God, and I trust in him (Psalm 91:1–2 NLT).

7. The LORD replied, "I will personally go with you, Moses, and I will give you rest—everything will be fine for you" (Exodus 33:14 NLT).

8. You, LORD, give true peace to those who depend on you, because they trust you (Isaiah 26:3 NCV).

9. Don't worry about anything; instead pray about everything. Tell God what you need and thank him for all he has done. Then you will experience God's peace, which exceeds anything we understand. His peace will guard your hearts and minds as you live in Christ Jesus (Philippians 4:6–7 NLT).

10. I find rest in God; only He can save me. He is my rock and my salvation. He is my defender; I will not be defeated (Psalm 62:1–2 NCV).

11. I said to myself, "Relax and rest. God has showered you with blessings. Soul, you've been rescued from death; Eye, you've been rescued from tears; And you, Foot, were kept from stumbling" (Psalm 116:7–8 MSG).

12. I will refresh the weary and satisfy the faint (Jeremiah 31:25 NIV).

13. He refreshes my soul. He guides me along the right paths for his name's sake (Psalm 23:3 NIV).

14. So repent [change your inner self, your old way of thinking, regret past sins] and return [to God; seek His purpose for your life], so that your sins may be wiped away [blotted out, completely erased], so that times of refreshing may come from the presence of the Lord [restoring you like a cool wind on a hot day] (Acts 3:19 AMP).

15. The law of the LORD is perfect, refreshing the soul (Psalm 19:7 NIV).

16. "Forget about what's happened; don't keep going over old history. Be alert, be present. I'm about to do something brand-new. It's bursting out! Don't you see it? There it is! I'm making a road through the desert, rivers in the badlands. Wild animals will say 'Thank you!'—the coyotes and the buzzards—because I provided water in the desert, rivers through the sun-baked earth, drinking water for the people I chose, the people I made especially for myself, a people custom-made to praise me" (Isaiah 43:16–21 MSG).

17. Don't think for a moment that you know it all, for wisdom comes when you adore Him with undivided devotion and avoid everything that's wrong. Then you will find the healing refreshment your body and spirit long for (Proverbs 3:7–8 TPT).

18. You're all I want in heaven! You're all I want on earth! When my skin sags and my bones get brittle, GOD is rock-firm and faithful. Look! Those who left you are falling apart! Deserters, they'll never be heard from again. But I'm in the very presence of GOD—oh, how refreshing it is! I've made Lord GOD my home. GOD, I'm telling the world what you do! (Psalm 73:25–28 MSG).

19. Finally, my brothers and sisters, rejoice! Strive for full restoration, encourage one another, be of one mind, live in peace. And the God of love and peace will be with you (2 Corinthians 13:11 NIV).

20. Restore to me the joy of your salvation and grant me a willing spirit, to sustain me (Psalm 51:12 NIV).

21. He had no beauty or majesty to attract us to him (Isaiah 53:2 NIV).

22. Heal me, LORD, and I will be healed; save me and I will be saved, for you are the one I praise (Jeremiah 17:14 NIV).

23. "For I know the plans I have for you," declares the Lord, "plans to prosper you and not harm you, plans to give you a hope and a future" (Jeremiah 29:11 NIV).

24. "But I will restore you to health and heal your wounds," declares the Lord (Jeremiah 30:17 NIV).

25. Instead of your shame you will receive a double portion, and instead of disgrace you will rejoice in your inheritance. And so you will inherit a double portion in your land, and everlasting joy will be yours (Isaiah 61:7 NIV).

26. Then the Lord your God will rescue you from your captivity! He will have mercy upon you and come and gather you out of

all the nations where he will have scattered you (Deuteronomy 30:3 TLB).

27. "Our Father who is in heaven, Hallowed be Your name. Your kingdom come. Your will be done, On earth as it is in heaven. Give us this day our daily bread. And forgive us our debts, as we also have forgiven our debtors. And do not lead us into temptation, but deliver us from evil. [For Yours is the kingdom and the power and the glory forever. Amen]" (Matthew 6:9–13 NASB).

Appendix II:

21 Self-Care Ideas

1. **Encourage yourself:** The fact that you've survived whatever you've been faced with is enough to acknowledge your effort, and celebrate the progress you've made. Do your best to be loyal to yourself in the times when you feel defeated. Be there for yourself. You need to be able to count on yourself and to believe in yourself. Treat yourself and speak to yourself the way you would a good friend. Encourage yourself using the Word of God.

2. **Smile:** A real smile can quickly and naturally lift your spirits. It's like you're showing no fear and that, despite your circumstances, you'll be happy because you have Jesus on your side. Smiling also contributes to longevity, as it helps increase your well-being and general happiness. Smiling makes you more likeable and courteous, which yields wonderful results for yourself and others.

3. **Laugh:** While smiling boosts your happiness, laughing is a physical manifestation you're not perturbed by your situation because you know the one called "Abba Father." Like Sarah, with laughter you can boldly say God has your back. *"God has made laughter for me; everyone who hears will laugh over me"* (Genesis 21:6).

   Some of the simple ways I brought laughter back into my life after Bell's palsy, was to watch funny videos online and on DVDs, tune in to my favorite sitcoms and plays, listen to some comedy on the radio, and read jokes and quotes of the day. I also read entertaining children's books while spending time with my daughter.

4. **Play:** Dwelling on your present situation will keep you feeling sad, worried, and stressed, but tapping into your inner child can take your mind off your troubles. One of my friends encouraged me to volunteer in the toddler classroom at the

preschool where I worked. This was a breakthrough in my healing process. One child asked if I was now the class clown. I told her, yes, and every afternoon for one hour I changed out of my work clothes into a red clown suit and allowed twenty toddlers the joy of my crooked smile for thirty minutes. It was painful for me to flex my facial muscles, but seeing these innocent children take joy in something I thought was so painful made me smile from the inside out. For the first time, I saw that something good could come from my pain.

5. **Get creative:** Creativity is a powerful way we craft new and beautiful things. So, even when your situation feels out of control, harnessing your creativity will inspire you to make something wonderful. Coloring, painting, sewing, making crafts, or writing are all ways to create something you can be proud of. They allow you to put your difficult situation on the back burner.

Some of the world's greatest masterpieces have been borne out of pain, such as the paintings from Picasso's blue period. If you're having trouble stirring up your creativity, you can do something simple such as coloring. It's not just for kids; there are some beautiful adult coloring books out there that have been shown to reduce stress and anxiety. I have also designed an adult coloring book to help bring peace, healing, and restoration to your life and a profound closeness with God.

6. **Eat well and rest:** Except when we're fasting, it's not recommended that we go without food. Situations can make us lose our appetite, but eating healthy food is what gives us the physical ammunition to restore our body. In the Bible, Paul suggested this to the people on a sinking ship with him when they were afraid:

"Therefore, I urge you to take some food. For it will give you strength, for not a hair is to perish from the head of any of you." (Acts 27:34).

During my recovery from Bell's palsy and before I could eat solid food again, soups, mashed potatoes, avocadoes, and coconut water became my best friends. But I was careful not to binge eat. In addition to feeding the body with the right foods, we must carve out meaningful time to exercise and rest, one of the best ways to rejuvenate and restore a well-nourished body. In doing so, the seed of healing took root in my heart, and color began to come back to my cheeks. I was smiling again and have been smiling ever since.

7. **Give:** Giving to and investing in others is a sure way of taking the focus off yourself. Doing this will bring you inner joy and fulfillment as well. I loved giving to others while I was recovering because blessing others helped me see that it wasn't all about me. I started writing short inspirational messages and daily texted them to my girlfriends, encouraging them to build their faith in God. In doing so, I, too, was encouraged. As I did this, God, through His Holy Spirit, kept whispering into my spirit promises so grand that my faith grew as tall as a mountain.

8. **Practice self-care:** You need appropriate time for healing and recovery to be your best self. Self-care is not selfish; it's a vital part of the healing process. Self-care can be as simple as a warm bath or as extravagant as going to the spa. Take some time to focus on loving and nurturing yourself. Daily, I would affirm, *"I now release with joy every sickness, every disease, every pain, and every misaligned emotion from my body. I bless with love my being and welcome with joy my well-being. My body is healed, and I appreciate my body parts for their support in helping me to fulfill my purpose."* I still do that today. Love and appreciate the body God has blessed you with.

9. **Forgive:** Forgiving yourself and others gives you a peace that cannot be found in physical possessions or activities. Because I blamed myself for past painful experiences, I had to release the blame and regret, knowing that it wasn't my fault. I also had to forgive everyone who had looked down on and talked about me because of my condition. Release the negative emotions and burdens that come from guilt and hurt.

10. **Embrace peace:** It doesn't matter how loud the noise around you is; make sure it's not louder inside of you. *Watch over your*

heart, for from it flow the springs of life (Proverbs 4:23 NASB). Protect the personal peace of your heart, for in the absence of peace, turmoil abounds. But when you know the truth, the truth will set you free. Let His peace wash over you, cleansing away your doubt, fear, and anxiety.

11. **Activate your faith:** I spent many days in isolation and hopelessness. I began praying, reading, reciting God's Word and giving thanks, activating my faith in God's power to heal me of this illness, just like the woman with the issue of blood. Jeremiah 17:14 became one of my favorite prayers: *"Heal me, LORD, and I will be healed; save me and I will be saved, for you are the one I praise"* (NIV).

12. **Create an amazing space of love**: Share love often and willingly. You don't need to go into anyone's darkness to help them. The only way to lead others out of darkness is to hold your light high so they can see their way out.

13. **Reflect:** Take some time to reflect on what got you here without placing blame on or judging yourself. It's okay to hold yourself accountable and identify the behaviors that will help you to make better decisions in the future. Don't allow yourself or the Enemy to weigh you down with what you wish you had done differently. Always speak as encouragingly to yourself as you would to a dear friend going through trauma.

14. **Take Epsom salt baths:** I take Epsom salt baths, hugging myself and pampering myself with lotion to be therapeutic. I also practice praying the Word of God over my life and speaking these words of truth over my body, "I love you," reminding my soul that "God loves you more" and "You are enough." Know that you can, and will make it through this, and walk into your much brighter future with God. Determine that you are a changed person and that from this point forward you will protect and assert yourself.

15. **Decide today that your past will not define you:** Use these life threads to help others get through their trauma, too. Rise above the temptation to give up or feel as though there's no

hope left. If you have breath in your body, you have an opportunity to override every circumstance that makes you think life isn't worth living anymore. You have a chance now to use the power God has invested in you to take control of your life, take back your joy, and share it with the world.

16. **Develop a strong devotional life:** If you have thoughts of leaving the church as a result of the spiritual abuse you've experienced, don't be ashamed. This is an entirely normal reaction. At one point, I walked away from the church because it was difficult for me to trust God. I blamed Him and the clergy who were a representation of Him. It wasn't until after I started processing my trauma that I was able to begin my relationship with God anew.

17. **Choose to pursue a deeper relationship with God:** Recognize that His love will deliver you from the shame of your past. He will give you the strength and courage to overcome your defeat and to come out of the darkness once and for all. Through understanding who God is and how much He loves you, you'll find the ability to love and forgive yourself and your abuser(s).

18. **Refuse to play the victim:** God doesn't want us to walk around with the shame of what we've done or what's happened to us. He came to set the captives free, so let His redeeming power expel all guilt and shame from you. God knows the end from the beginning. Over time, you'll be able to separate your abuser from God and the church. God doesn't want to see you in pain. He wants to restore you and show you that He is sovereign, even in your tragedy.

19. **Remember, this isn't a journey you have to walk alone:** Many resources are available, such as counseling. The effects of abuse are damaging and isolating, and they invade every aspect of your life mentally, emotionally, spiritually, and physically. The effects remain long after the abuse has ended. It's therefore crucial for you to work through these emotions so they won't have power over you or keep you from fulfilling your purpose in Christ.

20. **Allow God to help you to overcome:** You are not too broken to be healed. God loves you and He wants you to heal and thrive beyond that abuse you've experienced. Rest in the Lord!

21. **Love yourself: You are love!** You were created in love and by love. Stay in the presence of God's genuine love, for His unconditional love will fill you up continually.

> *I am a living testimony of God's faithfulness. God is about transformation. As you allow Him to sift through your life experiences and transform your tears of shame to joyful freedom, your purpose will soar. You were born to make a difference. You have a God-given purpose that the world needs to see, hear, and feel. It's time for it to come forth. Today can be your new beginning.*

THE LORD'S PRAYER

"Pray, then, in this way:

'Our Father who is in heaven,

Hallowed be Your name.

Your kingdom come.

Your will be done,

On earth as it is in heaven.

Give us this day our daily bread.

And forgive us our debts, as we also have forgiven our debtors.

And do not lead us into temptation, but deliver us from evil. For Yours is the kingdom and the power and the glory forever. Amen.' "

Matthew 6:9–13 NASB

CPSIA information can be obtained
at www.ICGtesting.com
Printed in the USA
FSHW021447100120
65483FS

9 781733 296625